EMMANUEL JOSEPH

Radiant Resilience: Bouncing Back from Life's Hurdles

Copyright © 2025 by Emmanuel Joseph

All rights reserved. No part of this publication may be reproduced, stored or transmitted in any form or by any means, electronic, mechanical, photocopying, recording, scanning, or otherwise without written permission from the publisher. It is illegal to copy this book, post it to a website, or distribute it by any other means without permission.

First edition

This book was professionally typeset on Reedsy.
Find out more at reedsy.com

Contents

1	Chapter 1: The Anatomy of Resilience	1
2	Chapter 2: Embracing Change and Uncertainty	3
3	Chapter 3: The Power of Positive Thinking	5
4	Chapter 4: Building Strong Relationships	7
5	Chapter 5: Overcoming Adversity with Grace	8
6	Chapter 6: The Role of Mindfulness in Resilience	10
7	Chapter 7: Setting and Achieving Goals	12
8	Chapter 8: The Importance of Self-Care	13
9	Chapter 9: Resilience in the Workplace	15
10	Chapter 10: The Role of Purpose and Meaning	16
11	Chapter 11: Learning from Failure	18
12	Chapter 12: Cultivating a Resilient Mindset	19

1

Chapter 1: The Anatomy of Resilience

Resilience is the ability to adapt and thrive in the face of adversity. It's not about avoiding challenges but learning how to confront them with strength and grace. Understanding resilience begins with acknowledging our inner capabilities and recognizing the importance of a positive mindset. Each of us possesses the potential to bounce back from setbacks, but it's a skill that needs nurturing and practice.

Building resilience starts with self-awareness. By understanding our emotions, strengths, and weaknesses, we can better navigate life's hurdles. This involves reflecting on past experiences and identifying patterns in our responses to stress. Mindfulness and self-compassion are crucial in this process, allowing us to embrace our imperfections and view challenges as opportunities for growth.

Support systems play a vital role in developing resilience. Whether it's family, friends, or professional networks, having a reliable support system can provide the encouragement and guidance needed during tough times. Building and maintaining these relationships requires effort, but the rewards are invaluable. A strong support system can offer different perspectives, help us stay grounded, and remind us that we are not alone in our struggles.

Lastly, resilience is bolstered by a proactive approach to life. Setting goals, maintaining a sense of purpose, and continuously seeking personal growth are essential. By focusing on what we can control and taking deliberate actions toward our objectives, we can build a foundation of resilience that enables us to weather any storm.

2

Chapter 2: Embracing Change and Uncertainty

Change is an inevitable part of life, and learning to embrace it can significantly enhance our resilience. Rather than fearing the unknown, we can view change as an opportunity for growth and self-discovery. This mindset shift allows us to approach challenges with curiosity and openness, making it easier to adapt to new situations.

One of the keys to embracing change is flexibility. By developing a flexible mindset, we can adjust our expectations and plans as circumstances evolve. This involves letting go of rigid thinking and being willing to explore new possibilities. Flexibility also means being open to learning from our experiences, both positive and negative, and using those lessons to inform our future actions.

Cultivating a sense of adventure can also help us embrace change. When we approach life with a sense of wonder and excitement, we are more likely to see challenges as opportunities for growth. This adventurous spirit can inspire us to take risks, try new things, and step out of our comfort zones. By doing so, we build our resilience and expand our horizons.

Finally, maintaining a positive outlook is crucial when navigating change. Optimism doesn't mean ignoring difficulties; instead, it's about finding the silver lining in every situation. By focusing on the potential benefits of change and maintaining a hopeful attitude, we can build the resilience needed to thrive in an ever-changing world.

3

Chapter 3: The Power of Positive Thinking

Positive thinking is a powerful tool in building resilience. Our thoughts shape our perceptions and, ultimately, our reality. By cultivating a positive mindset, we can enhance our ability to cope with stress and bounce back from adversity. Positive thinking involves focusing on the good in every situation and maintaining an optimistic outlook, even in the face of challenges.

One way to develop positive thinking is through gratitude. Practicing gratitude involves regularly acknowledging and appreciating the good things in our lives. This simple habit can shift our focus from what's going wrong to what's going right, helping us maintain a positive attitude. Keeping a gratitude journal or expressing thanks to others can be effective ways to incorporate gratitude into our daily routine.

Another aspect of positive thinking is self-affirmation. By regularly affirming our strengths and capabilities, we can build confidence and resilience. This involves identifying positive qualities about ourselves and repeating affirmations that reinforce these qualities. Over time, self-affirmation can help counteract negative self-talk and boost our self-esteem.

Lastly, surrounding ourselves with positive influences can enhance our ability to think positively. This includes spending time with uplifting people, engaging in activities that bring joy, and consuming inspirational content. By filling our lives with positivity, we can create an environment that supports and nurtures our resilient mindset.

4

Chapter 4: Building Strong Relationships

Strong relationships are a cornerstone of resilience. The connections we form with others provide emotional support, encouragement, and a sense of belonging. By fostering healthy relationships, we can build a support network that helps us navigate life's challenges.

Effective communication is key to building strong relationships. This involves actively listening to others, expressing our thoughts and feelings clearly, and showing empathy. By communicating openly and honestly, we can strengthen our bonds and create a foundation of trust and understanding.

Another important aspect of building strong relationships is mutual support. Resilient relationships are characterized by a balance of giving and receiving support. By being there for others and allowing them to be there for us, we create a reciprocal dynamic that enhances our collective resilience. This involves offering help, encouragement, and a listening ear during difficult times.

Lastly, nurturing relationships requires effort and commitment. This means regularly checking in with loved ones, spending quality time together, and showing appreciation for their presence in our lives. By prioritizing our relationships and investing in their growth, we can build a network of resilience that supports us through life's ups and downs.

5

Chapter 5: Overcoming Adversity with Grace

Adversity is an inevitable part of life, but how we respond to it defines our resilience. Overcoming adversity with grace involves facing challenges with courage, patience, and a positive attitude. It's about finding strength in the midst of difficulty and emerging stronger on the other side.

One of the keys to overcoming adversity is maintaining perspective. When faced with challenges, it's important to keep the bigger picture in mind and avoid getting overwhelmed by the details. This involves recognizing that setbacks are temporary and that we have the ability to overcome them. By keeping a hopeful outlook and focusing on our long-term goals, we can navigate adversity with resilience.

Another important aspect of overcoming adversity is self-compassion. It's essential to be kind to ourselves during difficult times and avoid self-criticism. Self-compassion involves acknowledging our struggles, treating ourselves with care, and allowing ourselves to make mistakes. By practicing self-compassion, we can build the resilience needed to bounce back from setbacks.

Lastly, seeking support is crucial when overcoming adversity. Whether it's talking to a trusted friend, seeking professional help, or joining a support group, reaching out for support can provide the encouragement and guidance needed to navigate difficult times. By leaning on our support network, we can find the strength to overcome adversity with grace.

6

Chapter 6: The Role of Mindfulness in Resilience

Mindfulness is a powerful practice that can enhance resilience. By cultivating mindfulness, we can develop greater self-awareness, reduce stress, and improve our ability to cope with challenges. Mindfulness involves paying attention to the present moment with an open and non-judgmental attitude.

One way to practice mindfulness is through meditation. Meditation involves focusing on our breath, body sensations, or a specific object while letting go of distractions. Regular meditation practice can help us develop greater focus, clarity, and emotional regulation. By incorporating meditation into our daily routine, we can build the resilience needed to navigate life's hurdles.

Another aspect of mindfulness is mindful living. This involves bringing mindfulness into our everyday activities, such as eating, walking, and interacting with others. By being fully present in each moment, we can enhance our appreciation of life and reduce stress. Mindful living also involves letting go of judgment and accepting things as they are, which can help us develop greater resilience.

Lastly, mindfulness can be practiced through self-reflection. This involves taking time to reflect on our thoughts, feelings, and behaviors. By examining our inner experiences with curiosity and openness, we can gain insights into our patterns and develop greater self-awareness. Self-reflection can help us identify areas for growth and build the resilience needed to navigate challenges.

7

Chapter 7: Setting and Achieving Goals

Setting and achieving goals is a crucial aspect of building resilience. Goals provide direction, motivation, and a sense of purpose. By setting meaningful and achievable goals, we can create a roadmap for our personal growth and development.

One key to effective goal-setting is clarity. Clear goals are specific, measurable, achievable, relevant, and time-bound (SMART). By defining our goals with precision, we can create a clear plan of action and track our progress. Clarity also involves understanding our priorities and aligning our goals with our values and aspirations.

Another important aspect of goal-setting is flexibility. While it's important to have clear goals, it's also essential to remain open to change. Life is unpredictable, and our goals may need to be adjusted as circumstances evolve. By maintaining a flexible mindset, we can adapt our goals to fit changing situations and stay resilient in the face of obstacles.

Lastly, achieving goals requires perseverance and commitment. It's important to stay focused and motivated, even when faced with setbacks. This involves breaking our goals into smaller, manageable steps and celebrating our progress along the way. By staying committed and persevering through challenges, we can build the resilience needed to achieve our goals.

8

Chapter 8: The Importance of Self-Care

Self-care is a fundamental aspect of building resilience. Taking care of our physical, emotional, and mental well-being is essential for navigating life's challenges. Self-care involves prioritizing our needs, setting boundaries, and engaging in activities that promote our overall health and happiness.

One key aspect of self-care is physical well-being. This includes maintaining a balanced diet, getting regular exercise, and ensuring adequate sleep. Taking care of our physical health provides the energy and stamina needed to cope with stress and bounce back from adversity. It's important to listen to our bodies and make self-care a priority in our daily lives.

Another important aspect of self-care is emotional well-being. This involves managing our emotions, practicing self-compassion, and seeking support when needed. By acknowledging and processing our emotions, we can develop greater emotional intelligence, and engaging in activities that bring joy and fulfillment. Self-care also involves setting boundaries and saying no when necessary to protect our well-being. By prioritizing our emotional health, we can build the resilience needed to navigate life's challenges.

Lastly, self-care includes mental well-being. This involves managing stress, staying mentally active, and seeking help when needed. Engaging in activities that stimulate the mind, such as reading, puzzles, or learning new skills, can enhance mental resilience. It's also important to seek professional help if needed and to practice relaxation techniques, such as deep breathing or mindfulness, to manage stress.

9

Chapter 9: Resilience in the Workplace

Resilience is not only important in our personal lives but also in the workplace. Building resilience at work involves developing the skills and mindset needed to navigate challenges and thrive in a professional environment. This includes managing stress, adapting to change, and maintaining a positive attitude.

One key aspect of workplace resilience is effective stress management. This involves recognizing the sources of stress in our work environment and developing strategies to cope with them. Techniques such as time management, delegation, and relaxation exercises can help reduce work-related stress and enhance resilience.

Another important aspect of workplace resilience is adaptability. The workplace is constantly evolving, and being able to adapt to new situations and challenges is crucial. This involves staying open to learning, being flexible in our approach, and embracing change. By developing a growth mindset and viewing challenges as opportunities for growth, we can build the resilience needed to thrive in the workplace.

Lastly, maintaining a positive attitude at work is essential for resilience. This involves focusing on the positives, celebrating successes, and maintaining a hopeful outlook. By cultivating a positive work environment and building strong relationships with colleagues, we can enhance our resilience and create a supportive professional network.

10

Chapter 10: The Role of Purpose and Meaning

Having a sense of purpose and meaning in life is a crucial aspect of building resilience. Purpose provides direction and motivation, helping us navigate challenges and stay focused on our goals. By finding and nurturing our sense of purpose, we can build a resilient mindset that enables us to thrive in the face of adversity.

One way to find purpose is by identifying our passions and interests. This involves reflecting on what brings us joy and fulfillment and aligning our goals with these passions. By pursuing activities and goals that resonate with our values and interests, we can create a sense of purpose that drives us forward.

Another important aspect of finding purpose is contributing to something greater than ourselves. This involves engaging in activities that benefit others, such as volunteering, mentoring, or supporting a cause we care about. By making a positive impact on the lives of others, we can find meaning and fulfillment that enhances our resilience.

Lastly, maintaining a sense of purpose involves setting and achieving meaningful goals. This includes setting both short-term and long-term goals that align with our values and aspirations. By working towards these goals with determination and perseverance, we can build the resilience needed to

CHAPTER 10: THE ROLE OF PURPOSE AND MEANING

overcome challenges and achieve our dreams.

11

Chapter 11: Learning from Failure

Failure is an inevitable part of life, but it can also be a powerful teacher. Learning from failure is a crucial aspect of building resilience. By viewing failure as an opportunity for growth and self-improvement, we can develop the skills and mindset needed to bounce back from setbacks.

One key to learning from failure is reflection. This involves taking time to analyze our failures, identify the lessons learned, and apply those insights to future situations. By reflecting on our experiences with an open and non-judgmental attitude, we can turn failure into a valuable learning opportunity.

Another important aspect of learning from failure is resilience. This involves developing the mental toughness needed to persevere through setbacks and keep moving forward. By maintaining a positive outlook and focusing on our long-term goals, we can build the resilience needed to overcome failure and achieve success.

Lastly, seeking support is crucial when learning from failure. Whether it's talking to a trusted friend, seeking professional help, or joining a support group, reaching out for support can provide the encouragement and guidance needed to navigate difficult times. By leaning on our support network, we can find the strength to learn from failure and emerge stronger on the other side.

12

Chapter 12: Cultivating a Resilient Mindset

Cultivating a resilient mindset is an ongoing process that involves developing the skills and attitudes needed to navigate life's challenges. By embracing a growth mindset, maintaining a positive attitude, and staying open to learning, we can build the resilience needed to thrive in the face of adversity.

One way to cultivate a resilient mindset is through continuous learning. This involves staying curious, seeking new experiences, and being open to feedback. By continuously learning and growing, we can develop the skills and knowledge needed to navigate challenges and adapt to change.

Another important aspect of cultivating a resilient mindset is maintaining a positive outlook. This involves focusing on the positives, celebrating successes, and maintaining a hopeful attitude. By cultivating positivity, we can build the resilience needed to overcome setbacks and achieve our goals.

Lastly, staying connected to our support network is crucial for cultivating a resilient mindset. This involves building and maintaining strong relationships with family, friends, and colleagues. By staying connected and seeking support when needed, we can enhance our resilience and create a network of encouragement and guidance.

Resilience is a journey, not a destination. It's about continuously developing the skills and mindset needed to navigate life's challenges and bounce back from adversity. By embracing change, maintaining a positive outlook, building strong relationships, and staying connected to our sense of purpose, we can cultivate the resilience needed to thrive in the face of life's hurdles.

As you embark on your journey of resilience, remember that you are not alone. There are countless others who have faced and overcome challenges, and their stories can provide inspiration and guidance. By learning from their experiences and applying the principles of resilience in your own life, you can build the strength and determination needed to overcome any obstacle. Stay resilient, and let your inner light shine brightly in the face of adversity.

Book Description

Radiant Resilience: Bouncing Back from Life's Hurdles

In the face of life's inevitable challenges, how do some individuals manage to not only survive but thrive? "Radiant Resilience: Bouncing Back from Life's Hurdles" explores the essence of resilience and offers practical guidance on how to cultivate this invaluable trait.

Through twelve insightful chapters, this book delves into the anatomy of resilience, the power of positive thinking, and the importance of building strong relationships. It emphasizes the role of self-awareness, mindfulness, and self-care in enhancing our ability to adapt and flourish. Each chapter is filled with relatable stories, expert advice, and actionable strategies to help readers navigate adversity with grace and emerge stronger on the other side.

Whether you're dealing with personal setbacks, professional challenges, or simply seeking to build a more resilient mindset, "Radiant Resilience" provides the tools and inspiration needed to bounce back from life's hurdles. Embrace the journey of resilience and let your inner light shine brightly, no matter what obstacles come your way.

www.ingramcontent.com/pod-product-compliance
Lightning Source LLC
LaVergne TN
LVHW021055100526
838202LV00083B/6248